CURRENT STOCK MARKET GUIDE FOR BEGINNERS

Learn the Basics Of Stocks Market Investing: A Step-by-Step Guide For Beginners

Charles J.Howard

Chapter 1. Understanding the Stock Market............**4**

Overview of how the stock market functions............4

Importance of stock market knowledge for
entrepreneurs.. 7

Chapter 2. Core Concepts and Terminology............**10**

Explaining stocks, bonds, ETFs, and other
investment instruments...................................... 10

Linking these concepts to entrepreneurial principles..
21

**Chapter 3. Benefits and Risks for Entrepreneurial
Investors**... **26**

Advantages of stock market participation for
entrepreneurs.. 26

Managing risks associated with stock market
investments... 30

Chapter 4. Formulating Investment Strategies........ **32**

Aligning investment goals with entrepreneurial
aspirations.. 32

Strategies for diversification and risk management 38

Chapter 5. Market Analysis Techniques...................**46**

Introduction to fundamental and technical analysis 46

Utilizing tools and resources for stock analysis...... 52

Chapter 6. Investment Approaches...........................**60**

Long-term vs. short-term investment strategies...... 60

Exploring value investing, growth investing, and
more.. 66

Chapter 7. Building a Well-Balanced Portfolio........ **70**

Creating a diversified investment portfolio............. 70

Balancing risk and return for entrepreneurs............ 73

Chapter 8. Insights from Successful Entrepreneurs.78

How entrepreneurs approach and succeed in the
stock market...78

Real-life examples and case studies....................... 83

Chapter 9. Ethical Considerations in Stock Investing......90

Socially responsible investing for entrepreneurs..... 90

Ethical implications of investment choices............. 95

Chapter 11. Conclusion and Next Steps....................98

Summary of key takeaways.................................... 98

Guidance for entrepreneurs to start their stock market
journey.. 100

Chapter 1. Understanding the Stock Market

Overview of how the stock market functions

The stock market is a place where people can buy and sell shares of companies, which are also called stocks. A share represents a fraction of ownership in a company, and its price reflects the value of the company and its future prospects.

The primary function of the stock market is to facilitate the exchange of stocks between buyers and sellers. Buyers and sellers can trade stocks directly with each other, or they can use intermediaries such as brokers, dealers, or market makers, who help match buyers and sellers and execute transactions on their behalf.

The stock market also serves as a platform for raising capital for companies. Companies can issue new shares to the public through a process called an initial public offering (IPO), or they can sell existing shares to investors through a process called a secondary offering. By selling shares, companies can raise money to fund their operations, expansion, or innovation.

The stock market operates through various exchanges, which are organized markets where stocks and other securities are listed and traded. Some of the major stock exchanges in the world are the New York Stock Exchange (NYSE), the Nasdaq, the London Stock Exchange (LSE), the Tokyo Stock Exchange (TSE), and the Shanghai Stock Exchange (SSE). Each exchange has its own rules and regulations for listing and trading stocks, and its own system for matching orders and executing trades.

The prices of stocks are determined by the forces of supply and demand in the market. A stock price increase occurs when there is a greater demand for the stock than there is supply. When more people want to sell a stock than buy it, the price of the stock goes down. The price of a stock also reflects the expectations of investors about the future performance and profitability of the company, as well as the risk and uncertainty associated with the company and the industry.

The stock market is constantly changing and evolving, as new companies enter and exit the market, new technologies and innovations emerge, and new events and information affect the economy and the society. The stock market is influenced by various factors, such as economic indicators, political events, natural disasters, corporate news, earnings reports, analyst ratings, market sentiment, and investor psychology. The stock market can be volatile and unpredictable, and it can offer both opportunities and risks for investors..

Importance of stock market knowledge for entrepreneurs

Why Entrepreneurs Should Learn About the Stock Market

The stock market is not only a place where investors can buy and sell shares of companies, but also a source of valuable information and insights for entrepreneurs. Whether you are planning to start, grow, or exit your own business, having knowledge about the stock market can help you make better decisions and achieve your goals. Here are some of the reasons why entrepreneurs should learn about the stock market and how it can benefit their businesses or investment decisions.

- It can help you understand the value and potential of your own business. By learning how the stock market works, you can gain insights into how investors evaluate and compare different companies, what factors affect their valuation, and how they can increase their attractiveness and credibility in the market. This can help you set realistic and achievable goals for your business, as well as plan and execute effective strategies for growth and expansion. For example, you can learn how to improve your financial performance, optimize your capital structure, enhance your competitive advantage, and communicate your vision and mission to the market.

- It can assist you in raising money for your company. One of the ways that entrepreneurs can fund their businesses is by going public, which means selling shares of their businesses to the public through the stock market. This can provide a large amount of capital for the businesses, as well as increase their visibility and reputation in the market. However, going public also involves various challenges and risks, such as complying with regulations, disclosing financial information, and facing market fluctuations. Therefore, entrepreneurs need to have a good understanding of the stock market process, the pros and cons of going public, and the best timing and methods for doing so. For example, you can learn how to prepare your business for an initial public offering (IPO), how to choose the right exchange and underwriter, how to price and market your shares, and how to manage your investor relations.

- It can help you diversify your income and assets. Another way that entrepreneurs can benefit from the stock market is by investing in other companies or industries that are related or complementary to their own businesses. This can help entrepreneurs diversify their income and assets, reduce their dependence on a single source of revenue, and hedge against potential losses or downturns in their own businesses. However, investing in the stock market also requires careful research, analysis, and decision-making, as well as awareness of the risks and opportunities involved. Therefore, entrepreneurs need to have a solid knowledge of the stock market fundamentals, the trends and dynamics of different sectors and markets, and the best practices and tools for investing. For example, you can learn how to select and diversify your portfolio, how to analyze and interpret financial statements and ratios, how to use technical and fundamental analysis, and how to apply risk management and asset allocation techniques.

- It can help you exit your business. Finally, one of the ways that entrepreneurs can exit their businesses is by selling their shares to the public or to other investors through the stock market. This can allow entrepreneurs to realize the value of their businesses, as well as to pursue other opportunities or goals. However, exiting a business also involves various considerations and implications, such as taxation, legal, and emotional issues. Therefore, entrepreneurs need to have a good understanding of the stock market options, the advantages and disadvantages of each option, and the best practices and tips for doing so. For example, you can learn how to evaluate your exit options, such as a secondary offering, a merger or acquisition, or a buyout, how to negotiate and structure the deal, how to prepare and execute the transition, and how to deal with the post-exit challenges and opportunities.

Conclusion

The stock market is a vital and vibrant part of the global economy, which provides opportunities and challenges for investors, entrepreneurs, and consumers. The stock market works by enabling the exchange of stocks between buyers and sellers, by providing a platform for raising capital for companies, and by determining the prices of stocks based on supply and demand and other factors. The stock market is also a dynamic and evolving phenomenon, which requires constant learning and adaptation from the participants. By understanding how the stock market works, entrepreneurs can gain a better insight into the world of finance and business, and make more informed and confident decisions.

Chapter 2. Core Concepts and Terminology

Explaining stocks, bonds, ETFs, and other investment instruments

What are Stocks, Bonds, ETFs, and Other Investment Instruments?

If you are interested in investing your money in the stock market, you may have heard of terms such as stocks, bonds, ETFs, and other investment instruments. What does this mean, though, and how are these concepts different from one another? In this article, I will explain the basic concepts and characteristics of these common investment instruments, and provide some examples of each. I will also help you understand how these instruments function within the stock market context, and what are the benefits and risks of investing in them.

Stocks

Stocks are units of ownership in a firm, sometimes referred to as shares or equities. When you buy a stock, you become a shareholder of the company, and you have the right to receive a portion of the company's profits, assets, and voting power. The price of a stock reflects the value of the company and its future prospects, and it changes according to the supply and demand in the market.

Common stocks and preferred stocks are the two primary categories of stocks. Common stocks are the most prevalent type of stocks, and they give shareholders the right to vote on important corporate matters, such as electing the board of directors, and to receive dividends, which are payments made by the company to its shareholders from its earnings. However, common shareholders are also the last to be paid in case of bankruptcy or liquidation, after the creditors and the preferred shareholders.

Preferred stocks are a special type of stocks that give shareholders a fixed amount of dividends, which are usually higher than those of common stocks, and a priority claim on the assets of the business in the event of bankruptcy or liquidation. However, preferred shareholders usually do not have voting rights, and their dividends may be skipped or suspended by the company if it faces financial difficulties.

Some examples of companies that issue stocks are Apple, Microsoft, Amazon, Tesla, and Coca-Cola. You can buy and sell stocks through brokers, dealers, or online platforms, and you can trade them on various exchanges, such as the New York Stock Exchange (NYSE), the Nasdaq, or the London Stock Exchange (LSE).

The benefits of investing in stocks are that they can offer high returns in the long term, as the company grows and increases its value and earnings, and that they can provide income through dividends. The risks of investing in stocks are that they can be volatile and unpredictable, as the price of a stock can fluctuate significantly due to various factors, such as economic conditions, corporate news, market sentiment, and investor psychology, and that they can result in losses if the company performs poorly or goes bankrupt.

Bonds

Bonds, also known as fixed-income securities, are debt instruments that represent a loan from an investor to a borrower, such as a corporation, a government, or a municipality. When you buy a bond, you lend your money to the borrower for a certain period of time, and you receive interest payments, also known as coupons, at regular intervals, and the principal amount, also known as the face value, at the maturity date, which is the date when the bond expires and the loan is repaid.

There are different types of bonds, depending on the issuer, the maturity, the interest rate, and the credit quality. ***Several typical bond kinds include:***

Corporate bonds, which are issued by corporations to raise funds for their operations, expansion, or innovation. Corporate bonds typically have higher interest rates than government bonds, as they carry higher risk of default, which is the failure to pay back the principal or the interest on time.

Government bonds, which are issued by national governments to finance their budget deficits, public spending, or debt obligations. Government bonds typically have lower interest rates than corporate bonds, as they are considered safer and more reliable, especially if they are issued by stable and creditworthy countries.

Municipal bonds, which are issued by state or local governments or their agencies to fund public projects, such as infrastructure, education, or health care. Municipal bonds usually have lower interest rates than corporate bonds, as they are exempt from federal and sometimes state and local taxes, making them attractive for investors in high tax brackets.

Treasury bonds, which are a specific type of government bonds issued by the US Treasury Department. Treasury bonds have a maturity of more than 10 years, and they pay interest semiannually. Treasury bonds are considered the safest and most liquid type of bonds, as they are backed by the full faith and credit of the US government, and they can readily purchased and sold in the marketplace.

Zero-coupon bonds, which are bonds that do not pay interest, but are sold at a discount to their face value, and pay the full face value at maturity. Zero-coupon bonds have a longer maturity and a higher sensitivity to interest rate changes than regular bonds, making them more volatile and risky.

Some examples of bonds are the 10-year US Treasury bond, the 30-year UK gilt, the 5-year Apple corporate bond, and the New York City municipal bond. You can buy and sell bonds through brokers, dealers, or online platforms, and you can trade them on various markets, such as the over-the-counter (OTC) market, which is a decentralized and informal network of buyers and sellers, or the bond exchange, which is a centralized and regulated platform for listing and trading bonds.

The benefits of investing in bonds are that they can provide steady and predictable income through interest payments, and that they can reduce the risk and volatility of your portfolio, as they tend to have a negative or low correlation with stocks, meaning that they move in opposite or different directions. The risks of investing in bonds are that they can have lower returns than stocks in the long term, as they have lower growth potential and lower interest rates, and that they can be affected by various factors, such as inflation, interest rate changes, credit rating changes, and default risk.

ETFs

ETFs, or exchange-traded funds, are funds that hold a collection of assets, such as stocks, bonds, commodities, currencies, or derivatives, and that trade on an exchange like a stock. When you buy an ETF, you buy a share of the fund, and you gain exposure to the performance and characteristics of the underlying assets.

There are different types of ETFs, depending on the strategy, the objective, the asset class, and the index that they follow. *Some of the common types of ETFs are:*

Index ETFs, which are ETFs that track and replicate the performance of a specific index, such as the S&P 500, the Dow Jones Industrial Average, or the Nasdaq 100. Index ETFs aim to provide the same returns and risk as the index, minus the fees and expenses of the fund.

Active ETFs, which are ETFs that do not follow an index, but use active management and research to select and adjust the assets in the fund, based on various criteria, such as value, growth, quality, or momentum. Active ETFs aim to outperform the market or a benchmark, by taking advantage of market opportunities and inefficiencies.

Sector ETFs, which are ETFs that focus on a specific sector or industry of the economy, such as technology, health care, energy, or consumer staples. Sector ETFs allow investors to target and benefit from the growth and trends of a particular sector or industry, as well as to diversify and hedge their portfolio.

Commodity ETFs, which are ETFs that invest in physical commodities, such as gold, silver, oil, or wheat, or in futures and options contracts that derive their value from the price of commodities. Commodity ETFs allow investors to gain exposure to the price movements and demand and supply dynamics of commodities, as well as to diversify and hedge their portfolio.

Inverse ETFs, which are ETFs that use derivatives and leverage to provide the opposite returns of an index or an asset class. Inverse ETFs allow investors to profit from the decline or the underperformance of the market or an asset class, as well as to hedge their portfolio.

Some examples of ETFs are the SPDR S&P 500 ETF (SPY), which tracks the S&P 500 index, the ARK Innovation ETF (ARKK), which uses active management to invest in disruptive and innovative companies, the Technology Select Sector SPDR Fund (XLK), which focuses on the technology sector, the SPDR Gold Shares (GLD), which invests in physical gold, and the ProShares Short S&P 500 (SH), which provides the inverse returns of the S&P 500 index. You can buy and sell ETFs through brokers, dealers, or online platforms, and you can trade them on various exchanges, such as the NYSE Arca, the Nasdaq, or the Cboe BZX Exchange.

The benefits of investing in ETFs are that they can offer diversification and exposure to a wide range of assets, sectors, and strategies, that they can have lower fees and expenses than mutual funds, which are another type of funds that hold a collection of assets, but that trade only at the end of the day, and that they can have higher liquidity and transparency than mutual funds, as they trade throughout the day and disclose their holdings and prices regularly. The risks of investing in ETFs are that they can have tracking error, which is the difference between the performance of the ETF and the performance of the index or the asset class that it follows, that they can have market risk, which is the risk of losing money due to the fluctuations of the market or the asset class, and that they can have specific risks, depending on the type of ETF, such as leverage risk, commodity risk, or currency risk.

Some of the other types of investment instruments that you can use to invest your money in the stock market are:

Options, which are contracts that give the buyer the right, but not the obligation, to buy or sell an underlying asset, such as a stock, a bond, or an ETF, at a specified price, called the strike price, within a specified period of time, called the expiration date. Options allow investors to speculate on the direction and magnitude of the price movements of the underlying asset, as well as to hedge their portfolio against adverse market conditions. Options have two main types: call options, which give the right to buy the underlying asset, and put options, which give the right to sell the underlying asset.

Futures, which are contracts that obligate the buyer and the seller to exchange an underlying asset, such as a commodity, a currency, or an index, at a predetermined price, called the futures price, on a specified date, called the delivery date. Futures allow investors to lock in the price of the underlying asset, and to profit from the difference between the futures price and the spot price, which is the current market price of the underlying asset. Futures also allow investors to hedge their portfolio against price fluctuations and risks of the underlying asset.

Mutual funds, which are funds that pool money from multiple investors and invest it in a diversified portfolio of assets, such as stocks, bonds, or ETFs, according to a specific objective and strategy. Mutual funds are managed by professional fund managers, who make the investment decisions and charge fees and expenses for their services. Mutual funds allow investors to access a wide range of assets and markets, and to benefit from the expertise and experience of the fund managers. However, mutual funds also have drawbacks, such as lower liquidity, higher fees and expenses, and lower transparency than ETFs.

Cryptocurrencies, which are digital currencies that use cryptography and blockchain technology to create, store, and transfer value, without the need for intermediaries, such as banks or governments. Cryptocurrencies are decentralized, peer-to-peer, and global, and they have unique features, such as limited supply, anonymity, and immutability. Cryptocurrencies allow investors to participate in a new and innovative form of money and payment, and to potentially benefit from the high growth and volatility of the cryptocurrency market. However, cryptocurrencies also have challenges, such as regulatory uncertainty, security breaches, technical issues, and environmental concerns.

These are some of the common investment instruments that you can use to invest your money in the stock market. Each of these instruments has its own advantages and disadvantages, and requires different levels of knowledge, skills, and risk tolerance. Therefore, before you invest in any of these instruments, you should do your own research, analysis, and due diligence, and consult with a financial advisor if necessary. You should also diversify your portfolio, and invest only the amount of money that you can afford to lose. Investing in the stock market can be rewarding, but also risky, so you should be prepared for the ups and downs, and have a long-term perspective and a clear goal.

Linking these concepts to entrepreneurial principles

The concepts of stocks, bonds, ETFs, and other investment instruments are relevant and useful for entrepreneurs, as they can help them understand and apply various entrepreneurial principles. **Here are some of the ways that these financial tools can benefit entrepreneurs in their business ventures or investment strategies:**

- Stocks can help entrepreneurs learn about the value creation and value capture of their businesses, as well as the expectations and preferences of the market and the investors. By studying how the stock market works, entrepreneurs can gain insights into how to evaluate and compare different companies, what factors affect their valuation, and how to increase their attractiveness and credibility in the market. This can help entrepreneurs set realistic and achievable goals for their businesses, as well as plan and execute effective strategies for growth and expansion. For example, entrepreneurs can learn how to improve their financial performance, optimize their capital structure, enhance their competitive advantage, and communicate their vision and mission to the market. Additionally, stocks can also help entrepreneurs raise capital for their businesses, by going public, which means selling shares of their businesses to the public through the stock market. This can provide a large amount of capital for the businesses, as well as increase their visibility and reputation in the market. However, going public also involves various challenges and risks, such as complying with regulations, disclosing financial information, and facing market fluctuations. Therefore, entrepreneurs need to have a good understanding of the stock market process, the pros and cons of going public, and the best timing and methods for doing so.

- Bonds can help entrepreneurs learn about the cost of capital and the risk-return trade-off of their businesses, as well as the debt financing and the credit quality of their businesses. By studying how the bond market works, entrepreneurs can gain insights into how to calculate and compare the cost of capital, which is the minimum return that investors require to invest in a business, and the risk-return trade-off, which is the balance between the potential return and the potential loss of a business. This can help entrepreneurs make optimal investment decisions, as well as manage and mitigate the risks of their businesses. For example, entrepreneurs can learn how to choose the best projects and opportunities for their businesses, how to diversify and hedge their portfolio, and how to deal with uncertainty and volatility. Additionally, bonds can also help entrepreneurs raise capital for their businesses, by issuing bonds, which means borrowing money from investors for a certain period of time, and paying interest and principal on time. This can provide a flexible and convenient source of capital for the businesses, as well as lower the tax burden of the businesses. However, issuing bonds also involves various challenges and risks, such as increasing the debt burden and the default risk of the businesses, and facing interest rate changes and credit rating changes. Therefore, entrepreneurs need to have a good understanding of the bond market process, the advantages and disadvantages of issuing bonds, and the best terms and conditions for doing so.

- ETFs can help entrepreneurs learn about the diversification and exposure of their businesses, as well as the market trends and opportunities of their businesses. By studying how the ETF market works, entrepreneurs can gain insights into how to diversify and expose their businesses to a wide range of assets, sectors, and strategies, and how to benefit from the growth and trends of the market and the economy. This can help entrepreneurs enhance the performance and potential of their businesses, as well as reduce the risk and volatility of their businesses. For example, entrepreneurs can learn how to target and benefit from the growth and trends of a particular sector or industry, such as technology, health care, energy, or consumer staples, how to access and explore new and emerging markets and regions, such as China, India, or Africa, and how to apply and leverage different strategies and techniques, such as value, growth, quality, or momentum. Additionally, ETFs can also help entrepreneurs invest in other companies or industries that are related or complementary to their own businesses, by buying and selling ETFs that hold a collection of assets, such as stocks, bonds, commodities, currencies, or derivatives. This can help entrepreneurs diversify their income and assets, reduce their dependence on a single source of revenue, and hedge against potential losses or downturns in their own businesses. However, investing in ETFs also involves various challenges and risks, such as tracking error, market risk, and specific risks, depending on the type of ETF. Therefore, entrepreneurs need to have a good understanding of the ETF market process, the benefits and risks of investing in ETFs, and the best practices and tools for doing so.

These are some of the ways that the concepts of stocks, bonds, ETFs, and other investment instruments relate to entrepreneurial principles, and how they can benefit entrepreneurs in their business ventures or investment strategies. By understanding and applying these financial tools, entrepreneurs can gain a better insight into the world of finance and business, and make more informed and confident decisions.

Chapter 3. Benefits and Risks for Entrepreneurial Investors

Advantages of stock market participation for entrepreneurs

Entrepreneurs are often motivated by their passion, vision, and goals, as well as by their desire to achieve financial independence and success.

One of the ways that entrepreneurs can overcome these challenges and achieve their goals is by participating in the stock market, which is a place where people can buy and sell shares of companies, which are also called stocks. By investing in stocks, entrepreneurs can not only increase their wealth and income, but also improve their skills and capabilities, and expand their opportunities and networks. **Here are some of the advantages that participation in the stock market offers for entrepreneurs:**

Potential returns: Investing in stocks can offer high returns in the long term, as the value and earnings of the companies grow and increase over time. Entrepreneurs can benefit from the capital appreciation of the stocks, which is the increase in the price of the stocks, as well as from the dividends, which are the payments made by the companies to their shareholders from their earnings. Entrepreneurs can reinvest their returns to compound their wealth and achieve their financial objectives, such as saving for retirement, education, or other purposes.

Access to capital: Investing in stocks can also provide access to capital for entrepreneurs, as they can use their stocks as collateral to borrow money from lenders, such as banks or brokers. Entrepreneurs can use the borrowed money to fund their own businesses, such as to start, grow, or expand their ventures, or to pursue other opportunities or projects. Entrepreneurs can also sell their stocks to raise cash when they need it, such as to pay off debts, cover expenses, or meet emergencies. For example, if an entrepreneur needed $50,000 to launch a new product, they could use their stocks as collateral to obtain a loan from a bank, or they could sell some of their stocks in the market to raise the cash.

Opportunities for business growth: Investing in stocks can also create opportunities for business growth for entrepreneurs, as they can learn from and network with other companies and investors in the stock market. Entrepreneurs can gain insights and knowledge from the performance and strategies of the companies that they invest in, as well as from the trends and dynamics of the market and the economy. Entrepreneurs can also establish and maintain relationships with other shareholders, managers, customers, suppliers, or partners of the companies that they invest in, and leverage their connections and resources to enhance their own businesses. For example, if an entrepreneur invested in Tesla stocks, they could learn from the innovation and leadership of Elon Musk, the founder and CEO of Tesla, as well as from the growth and potential of the electric vehicle industry. They could also network with other Tesla shareholders, managers, customers, suppliers, or partners, and explore possible collaborations or partnerships with them.

These are some of the advantages that participation in the stock market offers for entrepreneurs. By investing in stocks, entrepreneurs can not only increase their wealth and income, but also improve their skills and capabilities, and expand their opportunities and networks. However, investing in stocks also involves various challenges and risks, such as volatility, uncertainty, and loss of capital. Therefore, entrepreneurs should be careful and prudent when investing in stocks, and seek professional advice if necessary. They should also diversify their portfolio, and invest only the amount of money that they can afford to lose. Investing in the stock market can be rewarding, but also risky, so entrepreneurs should be prepared for the ups and downs, and have a long-term perspective and a clear goal.

Managing risks associated with stock market investments

Investing in the stock market can offer various benefits for entrepreneurs, such as potential returns, access to capital, or opportunities for business growth. However, investing in the stock market also involves various risks, such as volatility, uncertainty, and loss of capital. Therefore, entrepreneurs should be aware and prepared for these risks, and employ effective strategies or approaches to manage and mitigate them. **Here are some of the ways that entrepreneurs can manage the risks associated with investing in the stock market:**

Diversification: One of the most important and common ways to manage the risks of investing in the stock market is to diversify the portfolio, which means to invest in a variety of assets, sectors, and strategies, that have different characteristics and performance. By diversifying the portfolio, entrepreneurs can reduce the impact of any single asset, sector, or strategy on their overall returns and risk, as well as take advantage of the growth and trends of different segments of the market and the economy. For example, entrepreneurs can diversify their portfolio by investing in stocks, bonds, ETFs, and other investment instruments, that cover different industries, regions, and themes, such as technology, health care, energy, consumer staples, China, India, Africa, value, growth, quality, or momentum.

Research and analysis: Another way to manage the risks of investing in the stock market is to conduct thorough research and analysis of the companies, the markets, and the economy, before making any investment decisions. By researching and analyzing the financial performance, the competitive advantage, the growth potential, and the risk factors of the companies, as well as the trends and dynamics of the markets and the economy, entrepreneurs can gain a better understanding and insight into the value and prospects of their investments, as well as the opportunities and threats that they face. For example, entrepreneurs can research and analyze the financial statements, the ratios, the earnings reports, the analyst ratings, the news, and the sentiment of the companies, as well as the indicators, the events, the policies, and the forecasts of the markets and the economy.

Risk management and asset allocation: A third way to manage the risks of investing in the stock market is to apply risk management and asset allocation techniques, which means to measure and control the level of risk and return of the portfolio, and to adjust the proportion and distribution of the assets in the portfolio, according to the objectives and preferences of the entrepreneurs. By applying risk management and asset allocation techniques, entrepreneurs can optimize the performance and potential of their portfolio, as well as align their portfolio with their goals and risk tolerance. For example, entrepreneurs can apply risk management and asset allocation techniques, such as the Sharpe ratio, the beta, the standard deviation, the correlation, the efficient frontier, or the capital asset pricing model, to evaluate and compare the risk and return of different assets, sectors, and strategies, and to determine the optimal mix and weight of their portfolio.

Chapter 4. Formulating Investment Strategies

Aligning investment goals with entrepreneurial aspirations

Entrepreneurs are people who create, launch, and run their own businesses, by taking risks and pursuing opportunities in the market. Entrepreneurs are often motivated by their passion, vision, and goals, as well as by their desire to achieve financial independence and success. However, entrepreneurship is not an easy path, as it involves various challenges and obstacles, such as competition, uncertainty, and resource constraints.

One of the ways that entrepreneurs can overcome these challenges and achieve their goals is by investing their money in the stock market, which is a place where people can buy and sell shares of companies, which are also called stocks. By investing in the stock market, entrepreneurs can not only increase their wealth and income, but also improve their skills and capabilities, and expand their opportunities and networks.

However, investing in the stock market also requires a clear and coherent strategy, which aligns with the entrepreneurial goals of the individual or the business. Investing in the stock market without a strategy can lead to poor performance, wasted resources, and missed opportunities. Therefore, entrepreneurs should carefully plan and execute their investment goals in the stock market, to complement and support their entrepreneurial goals.

Here are some of the steps that entrepreneurs can take to align their investment goals with their entrepreneurial goals:

Define your entrepreneurial goals: The first step is to define your entrepreneurial goals, which are the specific, measurable, achievable, relevant, and time-bound outcomes that you want to accomplish with your business. Your entrepreneurial goals should reflect your passion, vision, and mission, as well as your strengths, weaknesses, opportunities, and threats. Your entrepreneurial goals should also be realistic and flexible, as they may change and evolve over time. For example, your entrepreneurial goals could be to launch a new product, to enter a new market, to increase your sales, to improve your customer satisfaction, or to exit your business.

Define your investment goals: The second step is to define your investment goals, which are the specific, measurable, achievable, relevant, and time-bound outcomes that you want to accomplish with your money in the stock market. Your investment goals should reflect your financial situation, your risk tolerance, and your time horizon, as well as your personal and professional preferences. Your investment goals should also be realistic and flexible, as they may change and evolve over time. For example, your investment goals could be to generate income, to grow your capital, to diversify your portfolio, to hedge your risk, or to fund your business.

Align your investment goals with your entrepreneurial goals: The third step is to align your investment goals with your entrepreneurial goals, which means to tailor your investment goals in the stock market to complement and support your entrepreneurial goals. This can help you optimize the performance and potential of your portfolio, as well as your business. **To align your investment goals with your entrepreneurial goals, you should consider the following factors:**

- **The type of assets**: You should choose the type of assets that match your entrepreneurial goals, such as stocks, bonds, ETFs, or other investment instruments. For example, if your entrepreneurial goal is to grow your capital, you may invest in stocks that have high growth potential and earnings, such as technology, health care, or consumer discretionary stocks. If your entrepreneurial goal is to generate income, you may invest in bonds that pay regular interest, or stocks that pay dividends, such as utilities, consumer staples, or real estate stocks. If your entrepreneurial goal is to diversify your portfolio, you may invest in ETFs that hold a collection of assets, such as index, sector, commodity, or inverse ETFs.

- **The sector or industry**: You should choose the sector or industry that matches your entrepreneurial goals, such as technology, health care, energy, or consumer staples. For example, if your entrepreneurial goal is to enter a new market, you may invest in the sector or industry that is related or complementary to your business, such as technology, health care, energy, or consumer staples. This can help you gain exposure and insight into the market, as well as to network and collaborate with other companies and investors in the sector or industry. If your entrepreneurial goal is to hedge your risk, you may invest in the sector or industry that is opposite or different from your business, such as utilities, consumer staples, or real estate. This can help you reduce the impact of any adverse market conditions or events on your business, as well as to take advantage of the opportunities and trends in the sector or industry.

- **The strategy or technique**: You should choose the strategy or technique that matches your entrepreneurial goals, such as value, growth, quality, or momentum. For example, if your entrepreneurial goal is to launch a new product, you may invest in the strategy or technique that focuses on innovation and differentiation, such as growth, quality, or momentum. This can help you learn from and emulate the performance and strategies of the companies that are innovative and differentiated, as well as to benefit from the growth and trends of the market and the economy. If your entrepreneurial goal is to exit your business, you may invest in the strategy or technique that focuses on valuation and profitability, such as value, quality, or momentum. This can help you evaluate and compare the value and profitability of your business, as well as to prepare and execute the transition and the deal.

These are some of the steps that entrepreneurs can take to align their investment goals with their entrepreneurial goals. By following these steps, entrepreneurs can create and implement a coherent and effective investment strategy in the stock market, which can help them achieve their financial and business goals. However, entrepreneurs should also be aware and prepared for the challenges and risks of investing in the stock market, such as volatility, uncertainty, and loss of capital. Therefore, entrepreneurs should also monitor and review their investment goals and their entrepreneurial goals regularly, and adjust them accordingly, as they may change and evolve over time. Entrepreneurs should also seek professional advice if necessary, and invest only the amount of money that they can afford to lose. Investing in the stock market can be rewarding, but also risky, so entrepreneurs should be careful and prudent when investing in the stock market, and have a long-term perspective and a clear goal.

Strategies for diversification and risk management

Diversification and risk management are two important and related concepts for entrepreneurs who want to invest in the stock market. In this article, we will explain what these concepts mean, why they are relevant for entrepreneurs, and how they can be applied effectively.

What is diversification?

Diversification is the process of investing in a variety of assets, sectors, and strategies, that have different characteristics and performance. By diversifying the portfolio, entrepreneurs can reduce the impact of any single asset, sector, or strategy on their overall returns and risk, as well as take advantage of the growth and trends of different segments of the market and the economy.

Why is diversification relevant for entrepreneurs?

Diversification is relevant for entrepreneurs for several reasons. First, diversification can help entrepreneurs enhance the performance and potential of their portfolio, as they can benefit from the positive returns of some assets, sectors, or strategies, while offsetting the negative returns of others. For example, if an entrepreneur invests in both technology and consumer staples stocks, they can enjoy the high growth and earnings of the technology sector, while mitigating the volatility and uncertainty of the consumer staples sector.

Second, diversification can help entrepreneurs reduce the risk and volatility of their portfolio, as they can lower the exposure and sensitivity of their portfolio to any adverse market conditions or events. For example, if an entrepreneur invests in both stocks and bonds, they can protect their portfolio from the fluctuations of the stock market, while earning steady and predictable income from the bond market.

Third, diversification can help entrepreneurs align their portfolio with their goals and risk tolerance, as they can adjust the proportion and distribution of their assets, sectors, and strategies, according to their objectives and preferences. For example, if an entrepreneur has a long-term and aggressive goal, they may invest more in stocks than in bonds, and more in growth than in value stocks. If an entrepreneur has a short-term and conservative goal, they may invest more in bonds than in stocks, and more in value than in growth stocks.

How to diversify effectively?

To diversify effectively, entrepreneurs should consider the following factors:

The type of assets: Entrepreneurs should choose the type of assets that match their goals and risk tolerance, such as stocks, bonds, ETFs, or other investment instruments. Each type of asset has its own advantages and disadvantages, and requires different levels of knowledge, skills, and risk tolerance. For example, stocks can offer high returns in the long term, but they can also be volatile and unpredictable. Bonds can provide steady and predictable income, but they can also have lower returns than stocks in the long term. ETFs can offer diversification and exposure to a wide range of assets, sectors, and strategies, but they can also have tracking error, market risk, and specific risks, depending on the type of ETF.

The sector or industry: Entrepreneurs should choose the sector or industry that matches their goals and risk tolerance, such as technology, health care, energy, or consumer staples. Each sector or industry has its own characteristics and performance, and is influenced by different factors, such as economic conditions, political events, consumer behavior, or innovation. For example, technology can offer high growth and innovation, but it can also be highly competitive and uncertain. Health care can offer high demand and stability, but it can also be highly regulated and complex. Energy can offer high potential and opportunity, but it can also be highly volatile and risky. Consumer staples can offer low volatility and reliability, but it can also have low growth and differentiation.

The strategy or technique: Entrepreneurs should choose the strategy or technique that matches their goals and risk tolerance, such as value, growth, quality, or momentum. Each strategy or technique has its own criteria and methods, and is based on different assumptions and expectations. For example, value focuses on finding undervalued and overlooked companies that have strong fundamentals and low prices. Growth focuses on finding fast-growing and innovative companies that have high earnings and high prices. Quality focuses on finding high-quality and consistent companies that have strong profitability and low debt. Momentum focuses on finding trending and popular companies that have high returns and high volumes.

What is risk management?

Risk management is the process of measuring and controlling the level of risk and return of the portfolio, and of adjusting the portfolio accordingly, to optimize the performance and potential of the portfolio. Risk management involves various techniques and tools, such as the Sharpe ratio, the beta, the standard deviation, the correlation, the efficient frontier, or the capital asset pricing model, that help entrepreneurs evaluate and compare the risk and return of different assets, sectors, and strategies, and to determine the optimal mix and weight of their portfolio.

Why is risk management relevant for entrepreneurs?

Risk management is relevant for entrepreneurs for several reasons. First, risk management can help entrepreneurs achieve their goals and objectives, as they can align their portfolio with their desired level of risk and return, and with their time horizon and liquidity needs. For example, if an entrepreneur has a long-term and aggressive goal, they may invest in a portfolio that has a high risk and a high return, and that can withstand the fluctuations of the market. If an entrepreneur has a short-term and conservative goal, they may invest in a portfolio that has a low risk and a low return, and that can be easily converted into cash.

Second, risk management can help entrepreneurs protect their portfolio from losses or downturns, as they can hedge their portfolio against adverse market conditions or events, and take advantage of the opportunities and trends in the market. For example, if an entrepreneur expects the stock market to decline, they may invest in inverse ETFs, which provide the opposite returns of the stock market, or in bonds, which tend to have a negative or low correlation with stocks, meaning that they move in opposite or different directions. If an entrepreneur expects the stock market to rise, they may invest in leveraged ETFs, which provide amplified returns of the stock market, or in stocks, which tend to have a positive and high correlation with the stock market, meaning that they move in the same or similar directions.

Third, risk management can help entrepreneurs improve their skills and capabilities, as they can learn from and adapt to the changes and challenges of the market and the economy, and make more informed and confident decisions. For example, if an entrepreneur encounters a market crash, they may learn from their mistakes and losses, and adjust their portfolio and strategy accordingly. If an entrepreneur encounters a market boom, they may learn from their successes and gains, and capitalize on their portfolio and strategy accordingly.

How to manage risk effectively?

To manage risk effectively, entrepreneurs should consider the following factors:

The risk-return trade-off: Entrepreneurs should understand and accept the risk-return trade-off, which is the balance between the potential return and the potential loss of the portfolio. Generally, the higher the return, the higher the risk, and vice versa. Entrepreneurs should not expect to achieve high returns without taking high risks, or to avoid risks without sacrificing returns.

Entrepreneurs should also not take unnecessary or excessive risks, or avoid risks completely, as both can be detrimental to their portfolio and their goals. Entrepreneurs should find the optimal level of risk and return that suits their objectives and preferences, and that they can afford and tolerate.

The diversification and exposure: Entrepreneurs should diversify and expose their portfolio to a variety of assets, sectors, and strategies, that have different characteristics and performance, as explained above. This can help entrepreneurs reduce the impact of any single asset, sector, or strategy on their overall returns and risk, as well as take advantage of the growth and trends of different segments of the market and the economy. However, entrepreneurs should also not over-diversify or under-expose their portfolio, as both can be detrimental to their portfolio and their goals. Entrepreneurs should find the optimal balance of diversification and exposure that suits their objectives and preferences, and that they can manage and monitor.

The research and analysis: Entrepreneurs should conduct thorough research and analysis of the companies, the markets, and the economy, before making any investment decisions, as explained above. This can help entrepreneurs gain a better understanding and insight into the value and prospects of their investments, as well as the opportunities and threats that they face. However, entrepreneurs should also not rely solely or blindly on the research and analysis, as they can be incomplete, inaccurate, or outdated. Entrepreneurs should also use their own judgment and intuition, and consult with professional advisors if necessary.

These are some of the ways that entrepreneurs can manage the risks associated with investing in the stock market. By following these steps, entrepreneurs can optimize the performance and potential of their portfolio, as well as their business. However, entrepreneurs should also be aware and prepared for the uncertainties and complexities of the market and the economy, and be ready to adapt and adjust their portfolio and their goals accordingly, as they may change and evolve over time. Entrepreneurs should also seek professional advice if necessary, and invest only the amount of money that they can afford to lose. Investing in the stock market can be rewarding, but also risky, so entrepreneurs should be careful and prudent when investing in the stock market, and have a long-term perspective and a clear goal.

Chapter 5. Market Analysis Techniques

Introduction to fundamental and technical analysis

Fundamental and technical analysis are two common and contrasting methods of analyzing and evaluating stocks in the stock market. Both methods aim to help investors make better and more informed investment decisions, but they differ in their approach, focus, and assumptions.

Fundamental analysis involves examining the financial performance, the competitive advantage, the growth potential, and the intrinsic value of a company, by using various sources of information, such as financial statements, earnings reports, analyst ratings, news, and industry trends. Fundamental analysis helps investors assess the financial health and future prospects of a company, and to determine whether the company is undervalued or overvalued by the market.

For example, if an investor wants to use fundamental analysis to evaluate Apple, a technology company that produces and sells various products and services, such as the iPhone, the iPad, the Mac, the Apple Watch, the AirPods, the Apple TV, the App Store, the iCloud, and the Apple Music, **they may look at the following factors:**

- The revenue, the earnings, the cash flow, and the margins of the company, which indicate the sales, the profitability, the liquidity, and the efficiency of the company.

- The assets, the liabilities, and the equity of the company, which indicate the resources, the obligations, and the ownership of the company.

- The ratios, such as the price-to-earnings ratio (P/E), the price-to-book ratio (P/B), the dividend yield, the earnings per share (EPS), and the return on equity (ROE), which indicate the valuation, the performance, and the attractiveness of the company.

- The competitive advantage, such as the brand, the innovation, the quality, and the loyalty of the company, which indicate the differentiation, the leadership, and the sustainability of the company.

- The growth potential, such as the market share, the market size, and the market opportunity of the company, which indicate the expansion, the penetration, and the diversification of the company.

By using these factors, the investor can estimate the intrinsic value of the company, which is the true and fair value of the company, based on its fundamentals, and compare it with the market value of the company, which is the current price of the company's stock in the market. If the intrinsic value is higher than the market value, the investor may conclude that the company is undervalued by the market, and that it is a good opportunity to buy the stock. If the intrinsic value is lower than the market value, the investor may conclude that the company is overvalued by the market, and that it is a good opportunity to sell the stock.

Technical analysis involves examining the price movements, the volume patterns, and the market trends of a stock, by using various tools and techniques, such as charts, indicators, oscillators, and patterns. Technical analysis helps investors identify and predict the direction and magnitude of the price movements and market trends of a stock, and to determine the optimal entry and exit points for trading the stock.

For example, if an investor wants to use technical analysis to evaluate Apple, **they may look at the following factors:**

- The price movements, such as the highs, the lows, the opens, and the closes of the stock, which indicate the fluctuations and the changes of the stock price over time.

- The volume patterns, such as the increases, the decreases, the spikes, and the gaps of the trading volume of the stock, which indicate the intensity and the interest of the trading activity of the stock.

- The market trends, such as the uptrends, the downtrends, and the sideways trends of the stock price, which indicate the direction and the strength of the stock price over time.

- The tools and techniques, such as the moving averages, the trend lines, the support and resistance levels, the Fibonacci retracements, the Bollinger bands, the relative strength index (RSI), the moving average convergence divergence (MACD), the candlestick patterns, and the chart patterns, which indicate the signals, the patterns, and the opportunities of the stock price movements and market trends.

By using these factors, the investor can analyze and forecast the price movements and market trends of the stock, and determine the optimal entry and exit points for trading the stock. For example, if the investor observes that the stock price is in an uptrend, that the trading volume is increasing, that the stock price is above the moving average, that the RSI is above 50, that the MACD is positive, that the stock price forms a bullish candlestick pattern, and that the stock price breaks above a resistance level, the investor may conclude that the stock price is likely to continue to rise, and that it is a good opportunity to buy the stock. If the investor observes that the stock price is in a downtrend, that the trading volume is decreasing, that the stock price is below the moving average, that the RSI is below 50, that the MACD is negative, that the stock price forms a bearish candlestick pattern, and that the stock price breaks below a support level, the investor may conclude that the stock price is likely to continue to fall, and that it is a good opportunity to sell the stock.

These are the concepts of fundamental and technical analysis in the context of stock market investing. Both methods have their advantages and disadvantages, and they can be used separately or together, depending on the preferences and objectives of the investors. However, both methods also require knowledge, skills, and experience, and they are not guaranteed to be accurate or successful. Therefore, investors should also use their own judgment and intuition, and consult with professional advisors if necessary. Investors should also diversify their portfolio, and invest only the amount of money that they can afford to lose.

Utilizing tools and resources for stock analysis

There are various tools and resources available for conducting stock market analysis, which can help entrepreneurs perform effective stock analysis, considering both fundamental and technical aspects. **Here are some of the tools and resources that entrepreneurs can leverage to analyze stocks and make informed investment decisions:**

Online platforms: Online platforms are websites or applications that provide access to various data, information, and tools for stock market analysis. Online platforms can help entrepreneurs find, compare, and monitor stocks, as well as to perform fundamental and technical analysis, using various sources and methods. **For example, some of the popular online platforms for stock market analysis are:**

- Yahoo Finance, which provides financial news, data, charts, indicators, and tools for stock market analysis. Yahoo Finance allows entrepreneurs to search and view the profiles, the financial statements, the ratios, the earnings reports, the analyst ratings, the news, and the sentiment of various companies, as well as to create and manage their own portfolio and watchlist of stocks. Yahoo Finance also allows entrepreneurs to perform technical analysis, using various tools and techniques, such as moving averages, trend lines, support and resistance levels, Fibonacci retracements, Bollinger bands, relative strength index (RSI), moving average convergence divergence (MACD), candlestick patterns, and chart patterns. Yahoo Finance can be accessed through its website or its mobile app.

- **TradingView**, which provides social networking, data, charts, indicators, and tools for stock market analysis. TradingView allows entrepreneurs to interact and learn from other traders and investors, as well as to share and publish their own ideas and opinions about the stock market. TradingView also allows entrepreneurs to perform fundamental and technical analysis, using various sources and methods, such as financial statements, ratios, earnings reports, analyst ratings, news, sentiment, charts, indicators, oscillators, and patterns. TradingView can be accessed through its website or its mobile app.

- **Stock Rover,** which provides research, data, charts, indicators, and tools for stock market analysis. Stock Rover allows entrepreneurs to perform fundamental and technical analysis, using various sources and methods, such as financial statements, ratios, earnings reports, analyst ratings, news, sentiment, charts, indicators, oscillators, and patterns. Stock Rover also allows entrepreneurs to screen and filter stocks, based on various criteria, such as value, growth, quality, or momentum, as well as to create and manage their own portfolio and watchlist of stocks. Stock Rover can be accessed through its website or its browser extension.

Software: Software are programs or applications that run on computers or devices, and that provide various data, information, and tools for stock market analysis. Software can help entrepreneurs perform advanced and customized stock market analysis, using various sources and methods, as well as to automate and optimize their trading and investment decisions. *For example, some of the popular software for stock market analysis are:*

- **MetaStock**, which is a software that provides data, charts, indicators, and tools for stock market analysis. MetaStock allows entrepreneurs to perform technical analysis, using various tools and techniques, such as moving averages, trend lines, support and resistance levels, Fibonacci retracements, Bollinger bands, relative strength index (RSI), moving average convergence divergence (MACD), candlestick patterns, and chart patterns. MetaStock also allows entrepreneurs to create and test their own trading systems and strategies, using various indicators, oscillators, and formulas. MetaStock can be downloaded and installed on Windows computers.

- **TradeStation**, which is a software that provides data, charts, indicators, and tools for stock market analysis and trading. TradeStation allows entrepreneurs to perform technical analysis, using various tools and techniques, such as moving averages, trend lines, support and resistance levels, Fibonacci retracements, Bollinger bands, relative strength index (RSI), moving average convergence divergence (MACD), candlestick patterns, and chart patterns. TradeStation also allows entrepreneurs to create and test their own trading systems and strategies, using various indicators, oscillators, and formulas, as well as to execute and monitor their trades, using various orders, alerts, and reports. TradeStation can be downloaded and installed on Windows computers, or accessed through its web platform or its mobile app.

- **Excel**, which is a software that provides data, charts, formulas, and tools for data analysis and manipulation. Excel allows entrepreneurs to perform fundamental and technical analysis, using various sources and methods, such as financial statements, ratios, earnings reports, analyst ratings, news, sentiment, charts, indicators, oscillators, and patterns. Excel also allows entrepreneurs to create and manage their own portfolio and watchlist of stocks, as well as to perform various calculations and simulations, using various formulas, functions, and macros. Excel can be downloaded and installed on Windows or Mac computers, or accessed through its web platform or its mobile app.

Data sources: Data sources are providers or repositories of various data, information, and statistics for stock market analysis. Data sources can help entrepreneurs access and obtain reliable and accurate data and information about the companies, the markets, and the economy, which can be used for fundamental and technical analysis. *For example, some of the popular data sources for stock market analysis are:*

- **EDGAR**, which is a database that provides access to the financial statements, the earnings reports, the filings, and the disclosures of the companies that are registered with the Securities and Exchange Commission (SEC), which is the US regulator of the stock market. EDGAR allows entrepreneurs to access and view the balance sheet, the income statement, the cash flow statement, the statement of equity, the notes, and the schedules of various companies, as well as to download and save the documents in various formats, such as HTML, PDF, or XML. EDGAR can be accessed through its website.
- **FRED**, which is a database that provides access to various economic indicators, statistics, and data for the US and the world. FRED allows entrepreneurs to access and view various indicators and data, such as the gross domestic product (GDP), the inflation, the unemployment, the interest rates, the exchange rates, the consumer confidence, the business confidence, and the trade balance, as well as to download and save the data in various formats, such as CSV, Excel, or PDF. FRED can be accessed through its website or its mobile app.
- **Quandl**, which is a platform that provides access to various financial and economic data and information from various sources, such as the

SEC, the Federal Reserve, the World Bank, the International Monetary Fund, the United Nations, and various exchanges, brokers, and analysts. Quandl allows entrepreneurs to access and view various data and information, such as the stock prices, the trading volume, the dividends, the splits, the earnings, the ratings, the news, and the sentiment of various companies, as well as to download and save the data in various formats, such as CSV, Excel, JSON, or XML. Quandl can be accessed through its website or its API.

Innovative technologies: Innovative technologies are new and emerging technologies that provide various data, information, and tools for stock market analysis. Innovative technologies can help entrepreneurs access and obtain novel and alternative data and information about the companies, the markets, and the economy, which can be used for fundamental and technical analysis. For example, some of the innovative technologies for stock market analysis are:

- **Blockchain**, which is a technology that uses a distributed and decentralized ledger to record and verify transactions and data, without the need for intermediaries, such as banks or governments. Blockchain can help entrepreneurs perform stock market analysis, by using various techniques and applications, such as smart contracts, tokens, and cryptocurrencies. For example, blockchain can help entrepreneurs access and obtain transparent and immutable data and information, such as the ownership, the transactions, and the performance of various stocks, as well as to execute and monitor their trades, using various orders, alerts, and reports, without the need for intermediaries, fees, or delays.

- **Big data,** which is a technology that uses large and diverse data sets, that are generated and collected from various sources and devices, such as the internet, the social media, the mobile phones, the sensors, and the satellites. Big data can help entrepreneurs perform stock market analysis, by using various techniques and applications, such as data mining, data analytics, data visualization, and data science. For example, big data can help entrepreneurs access and obtain novel and alternative data and information, such as the behavior, the preferences, the opinions, and the emotions of the customers, the competitors, and the investors, as well as to analyze and visualize the data and information, using various tools and methods, such as dashboards, charts, graphs, and maps.

These are some of the tools and resources available for conducting stock market analysis, which can help entrepreneurs perform effective stock analysis, considering both fundamental and technical aspects. By leveraging these tools and resources, entrepreneurs can access and obtain reliable and accurate data and information, as well as to analyze and interpret the data and information, using various sources and methods, and to make better and more informed investment decisions.

Chapter 6. Investment Approaches

Long-term vs. short-term investment strategies

Long-term and short-term investment strategies are two different approaches to investing in the stock market that differ in their time horizon, their objectives, and their methods. **Here are some of the differences between long-term and short-term investment strategies:**

Time horizon: The time horizon is the length of time that an investor plans to hold an investment, before selling it or realizing the returns. Long-term investment strategies have a longer time horizon, usually more than a year, and sometimes several years or decades. Short-term investment strategies have a shorter time horizon, usually less than a year, and sometimes a few months, weeks, days, or even hours.

Objectives: The objectives are the goals and expectations that an investor has for their investment, such as the level of return, the level of risk, and the purpose of the investment. Long-term investment strategies have a higher level of return, a lower level of risk, and a more strategic purpose, such as saving for retirement, education, or other long-term goals. Short-term investment strategies have a lower level of return, a higher level of risk, and a more tactical purpose, such as taking advantage of market opportunities, fluctuations, or inefficiencies.

Methods: The methods are the techniques and tools that an investor uses to select, analyze, and trade their investments, such as fundamental analysis, technical analysis, or other methods. Long-term investment strategies use fundamental analysis, which involves examining the financial performance, the competitive advantage, the growth potential, and the intrinsic value of a company, by using various sources of information, such as financial statements, earnings reports, analyst ratings, news, and industry trends. Short-term investment strategies use technical analysis, which involves examining the price movements, the volume patterns, and the market trends of a stock, by using various tools and techniques, such as charts, indicators, oscillators, and patterns.

For example, suppose an investor wants to invest in Apple, a technology company that produces and sells various products and services, such as the iPhone, the iPad, the Mac, the Apple Watch, the AirPods, the Apple TV, the App Store, the iCloud, and the Apple Music. The investor can use either a long-term or a short-term investment strategy, depending on their time horizon, their objectives, and their methods.

- If the investor uses a long-term investment strategy, they may hold the Apple stock for several years, and expect to achieve a high return, with a low risk, and a strategic purpose. The investor may use fundamental analysis to evaluate the financial health and future prospects of Apple, and to determine whether the company is undervalued or overvalued by the market. The investor may look at the revenue, the earnings, the cash flow, and the margins of Apple, which indicate the sales, the profitability, the liquidity, and the efficiency of the company. The investor may also look at the assets, the liabilities, and the equity of Apple, which indicate the resources, the obligations, and the ownership of the company. The investor may also look at the ratios, such as the price-to-earnings ratio (P/E), the price-to-book ratio (P/B), the dividend yield, the earnings per share (EPS), and the return on equity (ROE), which indicate the valuation, the performance, and the attractiveness of the company. The investor may also look at the competitive advantage, such as the brand, the innovation, the quality, and the loyalty of Apple, which indicate the differentiation, the leadership, and the sustainability of the company. The investor may also look at the growth potential, such as the market share, the market size, and the market opportunity of Apple, which indicate the expansion, the penetration, and the diversification of the company. By using these factors, the investor can estimate the intrinsic value of Apple, which is the true and fair value of the company, based on its fundamentals, and compare it with the market value of Apple, which is the current price of the company's stock in the market. If the intrinsic value is higher than the market value, the investor may conclude that Apple is undervalued by the market, and that it is a good opportunity to buy the stock. If the intrinsic value is lower than the market value, the investor may conclude that Apple is overvalued by the market, and that it is a good opportunity to sell the stock.

- If the investor uses a short-term investment strategy, they may hold the Apple stock for a few months, weeks, days, or even hours, and expect to achieve a low return, with a high risk, and a tactical purpose. The investor may use technical analysis to identify and predict the direction and magnitude of the price movements and market trends of Apple, and to determine the optimal entry and exit points for trading the stock. The investor may look at the price movements, such as the highs, the lows, the opens, and the closes of the stock, which indicate the fluctuations and the changes of the stock price over time. The investor may also look at the volume patterns, such as the increases, the decreases, the spikes, and the gaps of the trading volume of the stock, which indicate the intensity and the interest of the trading activity of the stock. The investor may also look at the market trends, such as the uptrends, the downtrends, and the sideways trends of the stock price, which indicate the direction and the strength of the stock price over time. The investor may also use various tools and techniques, such as the moving averages, the trend lines, the support and resistance levels, the Fibonacci retracements, the Bollinger bands, the relative strength index (RSI), the moving average convergence divergence (MACD), the candlestick patterns, and the chart patterns, which indicate the signals, the patterns, and the opportunities of the stock price movements and market trends. By using these factors, the investor can analyze and forecast the price movements and market trends of the stock, and determine the optimal entry and exit points for trading the stock. For example, if the investor observes that the stock price is in an uptrend, that the trading volume is increasing, that the stock price is above the moving average, that the RSI is above 50, that the MACD is positive, that the stock price forms a bullish candlestick pattern, and that the stock price breaks above a resistance level, the investor may conclude that the stock price is likely to continue to rise, and that it is a good opportunity to buy the stock. If the investor observes that the stock price is in a downtrend, that the trading volume is decreasing, that the stock price is below the moving average, that the RSI is below 50, that the MACD is negative, that the stock price forms a bearish candlestick pattern, and that the stock price breaks below a support level, the investor may conclude that the stock price is likely to continue to fall, and that it is a good opportunity to sell the stock.

These are the differences between long-term and short-term investment strategies in the stock market. Both strategies have their advantages and disadvantages, and they can be used separately or together, depending on the preferences and objectives of the investors. However, both strategies also require knowledge, skills, and experience, and they are not guaranteed to be accurate or successful.

Exploring value investing, growth investing, and more

There are various investment approaches, such as value investing, growth investing, and other prevalent methods in the stock market, that differ in their criteria, methods, and objectives. **Here are some of the investment approaches that investors can use to select and evaluate stocks:**

Value investing: Value investing is an investment approach that aims to find undervalued and overlooked companies that have strong fundamentals and low prices, relative to their intrinsic value. Value investors use fundamental analysis, which involves examining the financial performance, the competitive advantage, the growth potential, and the intrinsic value of a company, by using various sources of information, such as financial statements, earnings reports, analyst ratings, news, and industry trends. Value investors look for companies that have low valuation ratios, such as the price-to-earnings ratio (P/E), the price-to-book ratio (P/B), the dividend yield, the earnings per share (EPS), and the return on equity (ROE), which indicate the valuation, the performance, and the attractiveness of the company. Value investors also look for companies that have a margin of safety, which is the difference between the intrinsic value and the market value of the company, which provides a cushion against any errors in estimation or any adverse market conditions or events. Value investors believe that the market is inefficient and irrational, and that it often misprices the true value of the companies, creating opportunities for bargain hunting and long-term investing. Value investing was popularized by Benjamin Graham, who is considered the father of value investing, and his famous disciple, Warren Buffett, who is considered one of the most successful value investors of all time. Some examples of value stocks are Berkshire Hathaway (BRK.A), Walmart (WMT), and Coca-Cola (KO).

Growth investing: Growth investing is an investment approach that aims to find fast-growing and innovative companies, that have high earnings and high prices, relative to their intrinsic value. Growth investors use fundamental analysis, as well as other methods, such as qualitative analysis, which involves examining the vision, the mission, the culture, and the leadership of the company, by using various sources of information, such as interviews, surveys, reviews, and testimonials. Growth investors look for companies that have high growth rates, such as the revenue growth, the earnings growth, the cash flow growth, and the market share growth, which indicate the expansion, the penetration, and the diversification of the company. Growth investors also look for companies that have high growth potential, such as the market size, the market opportunity, and the competitive advantage of the company, which indicate the innovation, the differentiation, and the sustainability of the company. Growth investors believe that the market is efficient and rational, and that it often prices the true value of the companies, creating opportunities for capital appreciation and short-term investing. Growth investing was popularized by Thomas Rowe Price Jr., who is considered the father of growth investing, and his famous disciple, Philip Fisher, who is considered one of the most influential growth investors of all time. Some examples of growth stocks are Amazon (AMZN), Tesla (TSLA), and Facebook (FB).

- Other investment approaches: **There are other investment approaches, that combine or contrast the value and growth investing approaches, such as:**

GARP investing: GARP stands for growth at a reasonable price, and it is an investment approach that aims to find companies that have both growth and value characteristics, that have moderate earnings and moderate prices, relative to their intrinsic value. GARP investors use a combination of fundamental analysis and technical analysis, which involves examining the price movements, the volume patterns, and the market trends of a stock, by using various tools and techniques, such as charts, indicators, oscillators, and patterns. GARP investors look for companies that have moderate valuation ratios, such as the PEG ratio, which is the price-to-earnings ratio divided by the earnings growth rate, which indicates the balance between the valuation and the growth of the company. GARP investors also look for companies that have consistent and sustainable growth, which indicates the quality and the stability of the company. GARP investing was popularized by Peter Lynch, who is considered one of the most successful GARP investors of all time. Some examples of GARP stocks are Apple (AAPL), Starbucks (SBUX), and Home Depot (HD).

Contrarian investing: Contrarian investing is an investment approach that aims to find companies that are unpopular and out of favor, that have low earnings and low prices, relative to their intrinsic value. Contrarian investors use various methods, such as behavioral analysis, which involves examining the psychology, the emotions, and the biases of the investors, by using various sources of information, such as sentiment, surveys, polls, and indicators. Contrarian investors look for companies that have low sentiment, such as the pessimism, the fear, and the panic of the investors, which indicate the undervaluation and the overselling of the company. Contrarian investors also look for companies that have high potential, such as the catalysts, the triggers, and the events that can change the perception and the valuation of the company. Contrarian investors believe that the market is inefficient and irrational, and that it often overreacts to the news and the events, creating opportunities for buying low and selling high. Contrarian investing was popularized by David Dreman, who is considered one of the most successful contrarian investors of all time. Some examples of contrarian stocks are Exxon Mobil (XOM), IBM (IBM), and General Electric (GE).

Chapter 7. Building a Well-Balanced Portfolio

Creating a diversified investment portfolio

A diversified investment portfolio is a collection of different types of investments, such as stocks, bonds, ETFs, or other investment instruments, that have different characteristics and performance. A diversified investment portfolio is important for entrepreneurs who want to invest in the stock market, as it can help them achieve various benefits, such as:

Reducing overall risk: By investing in a variety of assets, sectors, and strategies, entrepreneurs can reduce the impact of any single asset, sector, or strategy on their overall returns and risk, as well as lower the exposure and sensitivity of their portfolio to any adverse market conditions or events. For example, if an entrepreneur invests in both technology and consumer staples stocks, they can enjoy the high growth and earnings of the technology sector, while mitigating the volatility and uncertainty of the consumer staples sector. Similarly, if an entrepreneur invests in both stocks and bonds, they can protect their portfolio from the fluctuations of the stock market, while earning steady and predictable income from the bond market.

Enhancing potential returns: By investing in a variety of assets, sectors, and strategies, entrepreneurs can also take advantage of the growth and trends of different segments of the market and the economy, as well as benefit from the positive returns of some assets, sectors, or strategies, while offsetting the negative returns of others. For example, if an entrepreneur invests in both value and growth stocks, they can benefit from the undervaluation and the appreciation of the value stocks, as well as from the innovation and the differentiation of the growth stocks. Similarly, if an entrepreneur invests in both domestic and international stocks, they can benefit from the stability and the opportunity of the domestic market, as well as from the diversification and the potential of the international market.

To manage a diversified portfolio, entrepreneurs should also monitor and review their portfolio regularly, and adjust it accordingly, as their goals, risk tolerance, and market conditions may change over time. Entrepreneurs should also seek professional advice if necessary, and invest only the amount of money that they can afford to lose. Investing in the stock market can be rewarding, but also risky, so entrepreneurs should be careful and prudent when investing in the stock market, and have a long-term perspective and a clear goal.

Balancing risk and return for entrepreneurs

Balancing risk and return is a crucial skill for entrepreneurs who want to invest their money wisely and grow their wealth. Risk and return are two sides of the same coin: the higher the potential return, the higher the risk involved. Entrepreneurs need to find the optimal balance between risk and return that suits their goals, preferences, and risk tolerance.

One strategy or method that entrepreneurs can employ to balance risk and return is diversification. Diversification means spreading the investment across different asset classes, sectors, industries, countries, and companies. This way, the entrepreneur can reduce the exposure to any single source of risk and benefit from the performance of various markets and sectors. Diversification can help entrepreneurs lower the overall risk of their portfolio without sacrificing the expected return.

Another strategy or method that entrepreneurs can employ to balance risk and return is asset allocation. Asset allocation means choosing the proportion of the portfolio that is invested in different asset classes, such as stocks, bonds, cash, real estate, commodities, etc. Each asset class has its own risk and return characteristics, and the optimal asset allocation depends on the entrepreneur's time horizon, risk appetite, and financial objectives. Asset allocation can help entrepreneurs align their portfolio with their risk and return expectations and adjust it over time as their needs and market conditions change.

To assess and manage the trade-off between risk and potential returns in the stock market, entrepreneurs need to measure and compare the performance of different stocks and portfolios. One way to do this is to use **risk-adjusted return measures or techniques**. Risk-adjusted return measures or techniques are methods that adjust the return of an investment or a portfolio for the amount of risk involved. They help entrepreneurs compare the performance of different investments or portfolios on an equal footing, taking into account both the return and the risk. **Some examples of risk-adjusted return measures or techniques are:**

Sharpe ratio: The Sharpe ratio measures the excess return per unit of risk of an investment or a portfolio. It is calculated by subtracting the risk-free rate (such as the interest rate of a treasury bill) from the return of the investment or the portfolio and dividing it by the standard deviation of the return. The risk-adjusted return improves with a higher Sharpe ratio.

Sortino ratio: The Sortino ratio is similar to the Sharpe ratio, but it only considers the downside risk of an investment or a portfolio. It is calculated by subtracting the minimum acceptable return (such as the inflation rate or the investor's target return) from the return of the investment or the portfolio and dividing it by the downside deviation of the return. The downside deviation is the standard deviation of the negative returns only. The higher the Sortino ratio, the better the risk-adjusted return.

Treynor ratio: The Treynor ratio measures the excess return per unit of systematic risk of an investment or a portfolio. It is calculated by subtracting the risk-free rate from the return of the investment or the portfolio and dividing it by the beta of the investment or the portfolio. The beta is a measure of the sensitivity of the investment or the portfolio to the movements of the market. The risk-adjusted return improves with a larger Treynor ratio.

To illustrate the concept of balancing risk and return, let us consider two hypothetical scenarios:

Scenario 1: An entrepreneur has $100,000 to invest and wants to achieve a high return in the stock market. He decides to invest all his money in a single stock that has a projected annual return of 20% and a standard deviation of 30%. His portfolio has a Sharpe ratio of 0.67, a Sortino ratio of 0.89, and a Treynor ratio of 0.2.

Scenario 2: An entrepreneur has $100,000 to invest and wants to achieve a moderate return in the stock market. He decides to invest his money in a diversified portfolio of 10 stocks that have a projected annual return of 10% and a standard deviation of 15%. His portfolio has a Sharpe ratio of 0.67, a Sortino ratio of 1.33, and a Treynor ratio of 0.1.

When we contrast the two situations, we observe that:

- The entrepreneur in scenario 1 has a higher expected return than the entrepreneur in scenario 2, but he also has a higher risk. His portfolio is more volatile and more exposed to the fluctuations of the market and the performance of the single stock. He may earn a high return, but he may also lose a large portion of his investment if the stock performs poorly.

- The entrepreneur in scenario 2 has a lower expected return than the entrepreneur in scenario 1, but he also has a lower risk. His portfolio is more stable and more diversified. He may earn a moderate return, but he may also preserve his capital and reduce his losses if the market or some of the stocks perform poorly.

- The entrepreneur in scenario 1 and the entrepreneur in scenario 2 have the same Sharpe ratio, which means that they have the same risk-adjusted return based on the total risk of their portfolios. However, the entrepreneur in scenario 2 has a higher Sortino ratio, which means that he has a higher risk-adjusted return based on the downside risk of his portfolio. He also has a lower Treynor ratio, which means that he has a lower excess return per unit of systematic risk of his portfolio.

Based on these comparisons, we can conclude that the entrepreneur in scenario 2 has a better balance between risk and return than the entrepreneur in scenario 1. He has achieved a similar risk-adjusted return with less risk and more diversification. He has also minimized his downside risk and his exposure to the market risk. He has optimized his portfolio's performance while managing risk.

Therefore, entrepreneurs can balance risk and return by using strategies or methods such as diversification and asset allocation, and by using risk-adjusted return measures or techniques such as Sharpe ratio, Sortino ratio, and Treynor ratio. By doing so, they can achieve their financial goals and grow their wealth in a smart and efficient way.

Chapter 8. Insights from Successful Entrepreneurs

How entrepreneurs approach and succeed in the stock market

The stock market is a challenging and competitive arena for entrepreneurs who want to grow their wealth and fund their ventures. Successful entrepreneurs employ various strategies and approaches when participating in the stock market, depending on their goals, preferences, and risk tolerance. **Some of the common strategies and approaches are:**

Long-term investing: Many entrepreneurs adopt a long-term investing approach, which means buying and holding stocks for years or decades, rather than trading frequently. This approach allows entrepreneurs to benefit from the compounding effect of reinvested dividends and capital appreciation, as well as to reduce transaction costs and taxes. Long-term investors also tend to focus on the fundamentals of the companies they invest in, such as their earnings, growth, competitive advantage, and innovation potential. Some examples of successful long-term investors who are also entrepreneurs are Warren Buffett, Jeff Bezos, and Mark Zuckerberg.

Value investing: Value investing is a strategy that involves buying stocks that are undervalued by the market, based on their intrinsic value. Value investors look for stocks that have a low price-to-earnings ratio, a low price-to-book ratio, a high dividend yield, or other indicators of financial strength and stability. Value investors also seek to buy stocks at a margin of safety, which means paying less than the estimated true value of the stock. Value investing requires patience, discipline, and research, as well as the ability to withstand market fluctuations and ignore short-term noise. Some examples of successful value investors who are also entrepreneurs are Benjamin Graham, John Templeton, and Charles Schwab.

Growth investing: Growth investing is a strategy that involves buying stocks that have high growth potential, based on their revenue, earnings, or cash flow. Growth investors look for stocks that have a high growth rate, a high return on equity, a high profit margin, or other indicators of competitive advantage and innovation. Growth investors also seek to buy stocks at a reasonable price, which means paying a fair multiple of the expected future earnings of the stock. Growth investing requires vision, creativity, and risk-taking, as well as the ability to identify and capitalize on emerging trends and opportunities. Some examples of successful growth investors who are also entrepreneurs are Thomas Rowe Price Jr., Steve Jobs, and Larry Page.

Diversification: Diversification is a technique that involves spreading the investment across different asset classes, sectors, industries, countries, and companies. Diversification reduces the exposure to any single source of risk and increases the chances of capturing the returns of various markets and sectors. Diversification also helps entrepreneurs balance their risk and return profile, as well as to align their stock market activities with their entrepreneurial endeavors. For example, an entrepreneur who runs a technology company may diversify their portfolio by investing in other sectors, such as health care, consumer staples, or utilities, to hedge against the volatility and uncertainty of the technology sector. Some examples of successful diversified investors who are also entrepreneurs are Oprah Winfrey, John Johnson, and Tom Love.

These are some of the strategies and approaches that successful entrepreneurs employ when participating in the stock market. However, there is no one-size-fits-all approach to investing, as each entrepreneur has their own unique perspective and specific traits that contribute to their success in the stock market. Some of these traits are:

Passion: Successful entrepreneurs are passionate about their businesses and their investments. They are driven by a vision and a purpose that motivates them to pursue their goals and overcome challenges. They are also passionate about learning and improving their skills and knowledge, as well as staying updated on the latest trends and developments in their fields of interest.

Curiosity: Successful entrepreneurs are curious about the world and the opportunities it offers. They are always looking for new ideas, insights, and information that can help them make better decisions and create value. They are also curious about the people and the problems they serve, as well as the feedback and the results they receive.

Persistence: Successful entrepreneurs are persistent in their efforts and their actions. They do not give up easily when faced with difficulties or failures, but rather learn from their mistakes and try again. They are also persistent in their pursuit of excellence and quality, as well as in their adherence to their principles and values.

Adaptability: Successful entrepreneurs are adaptable to changing circumstances and environments. They are flexible and willing to adjust their plans and strategies according to the market conditions and the customer needs. They are also adaptable to new technologies and innovations, as well as to new opportunities and challenges.

Real-life examples and case studies

Warren Buffett: Warren Buffett is one of the most famous and successful investors of all time. He is the chairman and CEO of Berkshire Hathaway, a conglomerate that owns and invests in various businesses, such as Coca-Cola, Apple, Bank of America, and Geico. Buffett is known for his value investing approach, which involves buying undervalued stocks that have strong fundamentals and competitive advantages. He also follows the principles of his mentor, Benjamin Graham, who taught him to look for stocks with a margin of safety, meaning that they are priced below their intrinsic value. Buffett has consistently outperformed the market and generated enormous wealth for himself and his shareholders. **Some of the key decisions and outcomes that illustrate his success in the stock market are:**

- In 1962, Buffett started buying shares of American Express, a credit card company that was facing a financial crisis due to a fraud scandal. He recognized that the company had a loyal customer base and a strong brand name, and that the scandal was only a temporary setback. He bought the shares at a low price and held them for years, earning a huge profit as the company recovered and grew.

- In 1988, Buffett began buying shares of Coca-Cola, a beverage company that was struggling with low sales and earnings. He believed that the company had a durable competitive advantage, a global presence, and a loyal customer base. He bought the shares at a reasonable price and held them for decades, reaping the benefits of the company's growth and dividends.

- In 2016, Buffett invested $1 billion in Apple, a technology company that was facing doubts about its innovation and growth prospects. He was impressed by the company's loyal customer base, strong brand name, and high profit margins. He increased his stake over time and became one of the largest shareholders of the company. He profited from the company's resurgence and dominance in the smartphone and wearable markets.

The valuable lessons or principles that aspiring entrepreneurs can learn from Buffett's success in the stock market are:

- Invest in businesses that you understand and that have strong fundamentals and competitive advantages.

- Invest in stocks long-term at a discount to their intrinsic worth.

- Ignore the short-term fluctuations and noise of the market and focus on the long-term performance and value of the businesses.

Jeff Bezos: Jeff Bezos is the founder and CEO of Amazon, the world's largest online retailer and cloud computing provider. He is also the founder and owner of Blue Origin, a space exploration company, and the owner of The Washington Post, a newspaper. Bezos is known for his growth investing approach, which involves buying stocks that have high growth potential and innovation. He also follows the principles of his role model, Thomas Edison, who taught him to experiment, innovate, and persevere. Bezos has transformed various industries and created enormous value for himself and his shareholders. **Some of the key decisions and outcomes that illustrate his success in the stock market are:**

In 1994, Bezos quit his lucrative job as a hedge fund manager and started Amazon, an online bookstore that later expanded into selling various products and services. He raised money from angel investors and venture capitalists, and took the company public in 1997. He reinvested the profits into expanding and improving the business, and diversified into new markets and segments, such as e-commerce, cloud computing, digital content, artificial intelligence, and smart devices.

In 2000, Bezos founded Blue Origin, a space exploration company that aims to make space travel accessible and affordable. He funded the company with his own money, and kept it secret for years. He pursued his vision of building reusable rockets and spacecraft, and competing with other players, such as SpaceX and NASA. He launched several successful test flights and missions, and plans to send humans to space in the near future.

In 2013, Bezos bought The Washington Post, a newspaper that was facing declining revenues and readership. He invested in the newspaper's digital transformation, and improved its technology, content, and distribution. He increased the newspaper's online presence and subscription, and enhanced its reputation and influence. He also supported the newspaper's journalistic independence and integrity.

The valuable lessons or principles that aspiring entrepreneurs can learn from Bezos's success in the stock market are:

- Invest in businesses that have high growth potential and innovation, and that can disrupt and dominate various industries and markets.

- Reinvest the profits into expanding and improving the business, and diversify into new markets and segments that align with your vision and passion.
- Experiment, innovate, and persevere, and do not be afraid to take risks and challenge the status quo.

Oprah Winfrey: Oprah Winfrey is a media mogul, philanthropist, and entrepreneur. She is the founder and CEO of OWN, a cable network and multimedia platform, and the chairwoman and CEO of Harpo Productions, a production company. She is also the host and producer of The Oprah Winfrey Show, a syndicated talk show that ran for 25 years and became one of the most popular and influential shows in television history. Winfrey is known for her diversification technique, which involves spreading her investment across different asset classes, sectors, industries, and companies. She also follows the principles of her mentor, Maya Angelou, who taught her to be authentic, compassionate, and generous. Winfrey has built a diverse and successful portfolio of businesses and investments, and created enormous value for herself and her shareholders. **Some of the key decisions and outcomes that illustrate her success in the stock market are:**

In 1986, Winfrey launched The Oprah Winfrey Show, a talk show that covered various topics, such as personal stories, social issues, health, spirituality, and entertainment. She negotiated a deal with King World Productions, a syndication company, that gave her full ownership and creative control of the show, as well as a share of the profits. She also founded Harpo Productions, a production company that produced the show and other projects, such as movies, documentaries, podcasts, and magazines.

In 2011, Winfrey launched OWN, a cable network and multimedia platform that features original programming, such as talk shows, documentaries, reality shows, and scripted series. She partnered with Discovery Communications, a media company, that provided the distribution and funding for the network, as well as a 50% stake in the venture. She also invested her own money and resources into the network, and became the chairwoman and CEO of the venture. She overcame the initial challenges and losses of the network, and turned it into a profitable and popular platform.

In 2015, Winfrey invested $43 million in Weight Watchers, a weight management company that offers products and services, such as diet plans, coaching, and online tools. She bought a 10% stake in the company, as well as a seat on the board of directors. She also became the spokesperson and the face of the company, and endorsed its products and services. She boosted the company's sales and stock price, and earned a huge return on her investment.

The valuable lessons or principles that aspiring entrepreneurs can learn from Winfrey's success in the stock market are:

- Invest in businesses that you are passionate about and that resonate with your audience and customers.
- Negotiate deals that give you ownership and control of your businesses and projects, as well as a share of the profits.
- Diversify your portfolio across different asset classes, sectors, industries, and companies, and leverage your brand and influence to add value to your investments..

Chapter 9. Ethical Considerations in Stock Investing

Socially responsible investing for entrepreneurs

Socially responsible investing (SRI) is an investing strategy that aims to help foster positive social and environmental outcomes while also generating positive returns. SRI is relevant to entrepreneurs in the stock market because it aligns with their values and objectives, and allows them to make a difference with their money.

Entrepreneurs are often driven by a vision and a purpose that goes beyond making profits. They want to create value for their customers, their employees, their communities, and the society at large. They also want to solve problems, address needs, and improve lives. SRI enables entrepreneurs to invest in companies and funds that share their vision and purpose, and that are engaged in social and environmental causes that they care about. For example, an entrepreneur who is passionate about clean energy and climate action may invest in companies and funds that promote renewable energy sources, reduce greenhouse gas emissions, and support green innovation.

SRI also helps entrepreneurs to consider the social and environmental impacts of their investment decisions, and to avoid investing in companies and funds that may harm their values and objectives. SRI encourages entrepreneurs to apply ethical and moral standards to their investments, and to avoid supporting businesses that are involved in activities that are detrimental to society and the environment, such as human rights violations, animal cruelty, pollution, corruption, or weapons production. For example, an entrepreneur who is committed to social justice and equality may avoid investing in companies and funds that discriminate against or exploit their workers, customers, or suppliers, or that contribute to social conflicts or injustices.

SRI can also benefit entrepreneurs financially, as there is evidence that socially responsible investments can perform as well as or better than conventional investments in the long term. SRI can help entrepreneurs to identify and capitalize on emerging opportunities and trends that are driven by social and environmental demands and preferences. SRI can also help entrepreneurs to reduce their exposure to risks and uncertainties that may arise from social and environmental issues and regulations. SRI can also enhance the reputation and credibility of entrepreneurs and their businesses, as they can demonstrate their commitment and contribution to social and environmental causes.

There are various ways that entrepreneurs can incorporate SRI principles into their investment portfolios, depending on their goals, preferences, and risk tolerance. **Some of the common ways are:**

Screening: Screening is a method that involves selecting or excluding investments based on certain social and environmental criteria. Entrepreneurs can use positive screening to choose investments that meet their SRI standards, or negative screening to avoid investments that violate their SRI standards. For example, an entrepreneur who wants to invest in companies that support gender diversity and inclusion may use positive screening to select companies that have a high percentage of women in leadership positions, or that offer equal pay and benefits to their employees. An entrepreneur who wants to avoid investing in companies that harm the environment may use negative screening to exclude companies that have a high carbon footprint, or that produce or use fossil fuels.

Thematic investing: Thematic investing is a method that involves investing in specific sectors, industries, or themes that are related to social and environmental causes. Entrepreneurs can use thematic investing to focus their investments on areas that they are passionate about, or that have high growth potential and impact. For example, an entrepreneur who is interested in health and wellness may invest in sectors or themes such as biotechnology, health care, organic food, or fitness. An entrepreneur who is concerned about water scarcity and quality may invest in sectors or themes such as water treatment, irrigation, desalination, or water conservation.

Impact investing: Impact investing is a method that involves investing in companies or funds that have a clear and measurable social and environmental impact, as well as a financial return. Entrepreneurs can use impact investing to support businesses or projects that are directly addressing social and environmental challenges or needs, and that are generating positive outcomes and changes. For example, an entrepreneur who wants to help alleviate poverty and empower marginalized communities may invest in companies or funds that provide microfinance, education, or employment opportunities to low-income or underserved populations. An entrepreneur who wants to promote sustainable development and biodiversity may invest in companies or funds that protect or restore natural habitats, or that support organic or fair trade farming.

Ethical implications of investment choices

Investment choices in the stock market have ethical implications that affect various stakeholders or societal aspects. Depending on the nature and impact of the investment decisions, the consequences can be positive or negative, intended or unintended, direct or indirect. Entrepreneurs should factor in these considerations while making investment choices, and be aware of the ethical responsibilities and impacts of their investment decisions.

Some of the potential consequences of investment choices on various stakeholders or societal aspects are:

Shareholders: Shareholders are the owners of the companies or funds that entrepreneurs invest in. They are entitled to a share of the profits and losses of the investments, as well as to have a say in the governance and direction of the companies or funds. The ethical implications of investment choices on shareholders are related to the financial performance, risk exposure, and reputation of the investments. For example, investing in a company that engages in fraudulent or illegal activities may harm the shareholders' interests, as they may face legal liabilities, financial losses, or reputational damage. On the other hand, investing in a company that adheres to high ethical standards and practices may benefit the shareholders' interests, as they may enjoy higher returns, lower risks, or positive recognition.

Employees: Employees are the workers of the companies or funds that entrepreneurs invest in. They are responsible for the production and delivery of the goods and services that the investments offer. The ethical implications of investment choices on employees are related to the working conditions, compensation, and rights of the workers. For example, investing in a company that exploits or abuses its workers may harm the employees' well-being, as they may suffer from low wages, poor benefits, unsafe environments, or discrimination. On the other hand, investing in a company that respects and empowers its workers may benefit the employees' well-being, as they may enjoy fair pay, decent benefits, safe environments, or diversity.

Customers: Customers are the consumers of the goods and services that the companies or funds that entrepreneurs invest in provide. They are the source of the revenue and feedback of the investments. The ethical implications of investment choices on customers are related to the quality, safety, and value of the goods and services that the investments offer. For example, investing in a company that deceives or harms its customers may harm the customers' satisfaction, as they may receive defective, dangerous, or overpriced products or services. On the other hand, investing in a company that delivers or enhances its customers' satisfaction may benefit the customers' satisfaction, as they may receive reliable, safe, or affordable products or services.

Society: Society is the collective of individuals and groups that interact and coexist with the companies or funds that entrepreneurs invest in. They are the context and the influence of the investments. The ethical implications of investment choices on society are related to the social and environmental impacts and outcomes of the investments. For example, investing in a company that contributes to social and environmental problems may harm the society's welfare, as they may cause pollution, climate change, poverty, inequality, or conflict. On the other hand, investing in a company that solves or mitigates social and environmental problems may benefit the society's welfare, as they may promote sustainability, conservation, development, justice, or peace.

Entrepreneurs should factor in these considerations while making investment choices, and be aware of the ethical responsibilities and impacts of their investment decisions. They should evaluate the ethical implications of their investment choices from multiple perspectives and dimensions, and weigh the trade-offs and consequences of their actions. They should also align their investment choices with their values and objectives, and seek to create value for themselves and others. They should also monitor and review their investment choices regularly, and make adjustments or corrections as needed. By doing so, entrepreneurs can practice ethical investing, which can help them achieve their financial goals and foster positive social and environmental outcomes.

Chapter 11. Conclusion and Next Steps

Summary of key takeaways

(1)The stock market is a place where investors buy and sell shares of companies that are publicly traded. Shares represent ownership of a fraction of a company's assets and earnings.

(2) Entrepreneurs can benefit from the stock market in two ways: by raising capital for their own ventures through an initial public offering (IPO) or by investing in other companies' stocks to diversify their income and grow their wealth.

(3) To raise capital through an IPO, entrepreneurs need to prepare a prospectus that outlines their business model, financial performance, growth potential, risks, and use of funds. They also need to hire an underwriter, a financial intermediary that helps them price and sell their shares to the public.

(4) To invest in the stock market, entrepreneurs need to understand the basics of stock analysis, valuation, and trading. Stock analysis involves researching the company's fundamentals, such as its earnings, revenue,

cash flow, and competitive advantage. Stock valuation involves estimating the fair value of a share based on its expected future cash flows or earnings. Stock trading involves buying and selling shares at the right time and price to maximize profits and minimize losses.

(5) Entrepreneurs should also be aware of the risks and challenges of the stock market, such as market volatility, liquidity, fraud, and regulation. They should have a clear investment objective, strategy, and plan, and follow some best practices, such as diversifying their portfolio, setting a stop-loss order, and keeping track of their performance.

(6) The stock market can be a rewarding opportunity for entrepreneurs who are willing to learn, research, and take calculated risks. It can help them raise funds for their own ventures, invest in other promising businesses, and achieve their financial goals.

Guidance for entrepreneurs to start their stock market journey

- Establishing your investment goals and objectives is the first step. What are you trying to achieve by investing in the stock market? How much money are you willing to invest and risk? How long are you planning to stay invested?

What is your risk tolerance and return expectation? These questions will help you clarify your purpose and motivation for investing, as well as guide your decision-making process.

- The second step is to learn the basics of the stock market and how it works. You need to understand the concepts of stocks, shares, dividends, market capitalization, indices, sectors, and industries. You also need to know the types of stock markets, such as primary and secondary markets, and the major stock exchanges, such as the New York Stock Exchange (NYSE) and the Nasdaq. You should also familiarize yourself with the terminology and jargon used in the stock market, such as bid, ask, spread, volume, volatility, and liquidity.

- The third step is to research and analyze the companies and stocks that you are interested in investing in. You need to evaluate the company's financial performance, growth potential, competitive advantage, and risks. You also need to compare the company's stock price with its intrinsic value, which is the estimated fair value of a share based on its expected future cash flows or earnings. You can use various tools and methods to conduct stock analysis and valuation, such as financial ratios, financial statements, earnings reports, analyst ratings, and valuation models.

- The fourth step is to choose an investment strategy and plan that suits your goals, objectives, and risk profile. You need to decide how much money you want to allocate to each stock, how often you want to buy and sell, and what criteria you will use to enter and exit a trade. You also need to diversify your portfolio across different stocks, sectors, and industries, to reduce your exposure to specific risks and increase your chances of earning higher returns. You should also set a stop-loss order, which is a predetermined price at which you will sell a stock if it falls below a certain level, to limit your losses and protect your profits.

- The fifth step is to open a brokerage account and start trading. A brokerage account is an account that allows you to buy and sell stocks through a broker, who is a person or a firm that acts as an intermediary between you and the stock market. You need to choose a broker that meets your needs and preferences, such as fees, commissions, services, platforms, and customer support. You also need to follow the rules and regulations of the stock market, such as trading hours, margin requirements, and tax implications.

- The last phase is to keep an eye on and assess your development and performance. You need to keep track of your portfolio's value, returns, and risks, and compare them with your goals and objectives. You also need to review your investment strategy and plan, and make adjustments as needed, based on your changing circumstances and market conditions. You should also seek feedback and advice from experts, mentors, and peers, and learn from your successes and failures.

Wishing success to every entrepreneur!